Copyright © 2008 by Bramcost Publications
All rights reserved
Published in the United States of America

This Bramcost Publications edition is an unabridged republication
of the rare original work first published in 1924.

www.BramcostPublications.com

ISBN 10: 1-934268-79-8
ISBN 13: 978-1-934268-79-7

Making a Dress in An Hour

By MARY BROOKS PICKEN
Director of Instruction
Woman's Institute of Domestic Arts & Sciences
Scranton, Pa.

A SMART, up-to-the-minute dress cut out, completely made, all ready to put on within an hour! You may receive a 'phone call at one o'clock inviting you to a little impromptu gathering of friends at three, and you can go, if you wish, wearing a dainty new frock made in the time you would ordinarily spend wondering what to wear.

Such is the delight you can find in making your own clothes now that it is easily possible to make an attractive, becoming dress in an hour.

And you can have as many "One Hour Dresses" as your heart desires—in infinite variety, for the "One Hour Dress" is not a *style* of dress, it is a *method of making*. It is a new and simple *plan* by which the dress you select from the many designs in this book can actually be cut out, put together, finished all complete in sixty minutes. And you can create other "One Hour Dresses" for yourself, because different combinations of colors and materials, different finishes and touches of decoration will enable you to have just the dress that appeals to your taste and have it quickly and at little cost.

Remember that to make a dress quickly you must first understand just what you are going to do—then do this step by step in a systematic way. So read the instructions carefully, observe the pictures and note their meaning. First be sure you understand—then go ahead and you can make the dress of your choice with surprising ease.

The One-Piece
One Hour Dress

Fig. 1

To follow the mode is delightful when it can be done so easily and economically as in the One Hour Dress.

The following pages tell you how to make up lovely silk or wool fabrics into beautiful frocks that are designed and cut without patterns—frocks that express the smartest lines and the newest trimmings in the very happiest way.

Dressmaking is difficult only when you hesitate because of lack of knowledge. Here we have explained every detail so that even though you do not sew, you should be able to make an attractive, creditable dress. And if you do sew, these instructions will be invaluable to you. Fig. 1 shows a smart, one-piece dress made of one of the new plaid flannels. Variations are shown on Pages 6 and 7.

Materials Required.—The 54-inch wool fabrics, such as flannel, wool crêpe, fine Poiret, or charmeen, cut to best advantage in this dress, though the 32-, 36-, or 40-inch material is satisfactory also. One length plus ¼ yard of the 54-inch material is sufficient; two lengths of the narrower widths are necessary, unless one chooses to use a tunic band at the bottom; then, one and three-fourth lengths are sufficient.

If 40-inch silk is used, a luxuriously long scarf may be made of the strip that is cut from the side.

Taking Your Measurements

Four measurements are required, and these are taken as shown in Fig. 2.

For your *blouse length*, put a pin in the dress you have on a little below your normal waist line or in line with the hip bones, to mark the waist line for the dress you are to make. If you are rather short, this is usually 2 inches below your normal waist line; if medium height, 3 inches; if tall, 4 inches. Measure from the pin in front, over the shoulder, and down the back to a point opposite the pin.

To obtain your *skirt length*, drop the end of the tape measure about 1 inch below the skirt length you want and measure from there to the pin. The extra inch will be taken up in the dart and the fitting at the waist line.

For your *hip measure*, measure around the hips at the fullest part.

For your *armhole measure*, measure around your arm at the shoulder, holding the tape moderately tight.

Fig. 2

Preparing the Material

After taking the measurements and before cutting the material, straighten the edges by cutting or tearing. If wool is used, tear or cut the material straight at both ends before shrinking it, and, if necessary to make it perfectly straight, pull it from the corners on the bias. All fabrics are woven straight, but in the folding they sometimes become crooked. Printed fabrics with large designs are the only kind that cannot be made satisfactory for cutting by tearing or cutting on a crosswise thread. These should be cut with regard to the design.

Cutting the Dress

Folding the Material.—First, lay out the material folded wrong side out through the center lengthwise, selvage edges toward you, as in Fig. 3, and pin along the fold. Measure half the distance from the lengthwise fold and put a pin, as at *a*, through both thicknesses of material. Then turn the top selvage up over the fold *b*, with the selvage itself extending beyond this fold. Turn over the folded material so that the other half is on top and bring the selvage edge down to meet the other selvage. Smooth the material out carefully and pin through both folds the full length of the piece, when the folded material will appear as in Fig. 4. This places the material so that the upper part, or fold, makes the front of the dress and the under part, or fold, the back, and brings the one seam on the left side.

Cutting the Neck Opening.—Next, locate the shoulder point at the neck by measuring down, or toward you, 2 inches from *c* at one end of the upper fold and marking *d*. Measure to the left on the upper fold 5 inches from *c* and locate *e*. Then cut on a straight thread from *c* to *e* to obtain the front-neck opening.

Shaping the Shoulders.—Now, to shape the shoulders, measure, for most figures, on the selvage to the left of the corner, or *f*, 3½ inches, and locate *g*. Very square shoulders require 2½ to 3 inches. Sloping shoulders require 3 to 4 inches. Then cut through the four thicknesses from *g* to *d* to make the shoulder line. A good plan is first to draw a chalk line along a ruler from *g* to *d* and then cut on this line to insure accuracy. Next, mark the width of the sleeves by measuring to the left from *g* one-half the arm-hole measure and placing a pin, as at *h*.

Cutting the Waist-Line Dart and Under Arm.—Now measure down from the shoulder line one-half the blouse length and over from the fold one-fourth the hip measure, plus 1½ inches, and locate *i*. Cut on a straight grain from the selvage

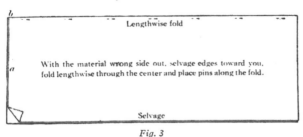

Fig. 3

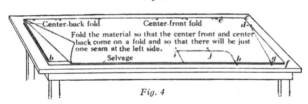

Fig. 4

edge in to *i* through all thicknesses. This gives the waist-line dart and provides for the plait.

Prepare the under arm by measuring straight to the right of *i* 8 or 10 inches and locating *j*. Then cut in a curved line from *h* to *j*, and straight down from *j* to *i*.

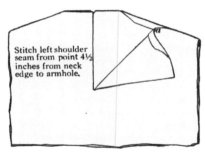

Fig. 5

Completing the Cutting.—Complete the cutting of the dress by removing the selvage from line *g h* and by slashing the fold on the undersleeve, doing this so that both sleeves are of the same length.

The neck is not shaped at this time, as it is advisable first to fit the collar at the neck and then to cut the surplus material away.

Making the Dress

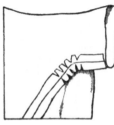

Fig. 6

Sewing Up the Seams.—Prepare to sew up the dress, which has five seams. Begin the right-shoulder seam at the neck edge and stitch out to the armhole, using a ⅜-inch seam. Begin the left-shoulder seam, as shown at *a*, Fig. 5, 4 inches down from the neck edge to allow for the opening. Stitch the curved under-arm seams, beginning at the edge of the sleeve and stitching around the curve and down to the waist-line dart. In doing this, keep the edges together accurately by means of pins or baste carefully so that the material will not slip.

Next, stitch the side seam of the skirt part, beginning at the waist-line dart and stitching down. When the seams are all stitched, clip the selvage edges every 6 to 12 inches to prevent their drawing; then clip the under-arm seams at the curve, as in Fig. 6, making about five clips in the turn, about 1 inch apart.

Pin the skirt plaits in place, allowing each to come toward the front or back, as you prefer, but with the outside edge of each in direct line with the under-arm seam.

Finishing the Neck Opening.—Finish the neck opening with stay tape or ribbon, as shown in Fig. 7, view (*a*) showing the right side and view (*b*), the wrong side. First clip the shoulder seam, as at *a*, view (*b*), so that the seam will lie flat, and then face the front edge with the tape or ribbon and bind the back edge. Make sure that the back-shoulder binding is as long as the front facing and take narrow seams so that the shoulder seam will not pull up.

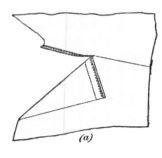

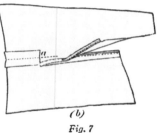

Fig. 7

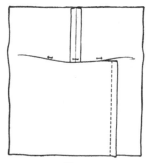

Fig. 8

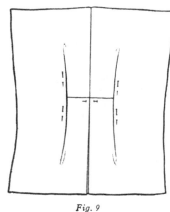

Fig. 9

Putting in the Hip Dart and Side Plaits. Pin in the dart, taking up ¾ inch of the material at the seam for the average figure and tapering it to nothing about 2 to 2½ inches on each side. On the wrong side, the dart will appear as in Fig. 8. Pin the hem up the amount allowed, turning an even line all the way around. The skirt length for this type of dress is determined by the hip dart, all fitting being done there. So turn the hem the amount allowed, evenly all the way, usually 3 to 4 inches.

At this time, it is advisable to slip the dress on to make sure that the darts are pinned to give an even line at the bottom, also that the hem is turned so as to make the skirt the correct length.

Pinch the side plaits in, as in Fig. 9, along both sides of the dart to get the effect desired. These plaits really fit the dress to the figure, controlling the fulness enough to make a belt unnecessary. However, one may be used across the back or front or all the way around, if desired.

Remove the dress, stitch the dart carefully, taking up just what was pinned in; then press the dart down, when from the wrong side it will appear as in Fig. 10. Turn the dress right side out, stitch the pinched plaits down, stitching ¼ inch from the edge and about 2 inches above the dart and 1 inch below.

Turn the dress wrong side out and prepare to stay the edge of the plait to the dart. First smooth the dress so that the plait will lie flat and on the straight of the material. Then take a few secure stitches, as at *a*, Fig. 10, to hold it firmly in position.

Finishing the Sleeves, Hem, and Neck.—Finish the lower part of the sleeves by using seam tape or ribbon. To do this, apply the tape to the right side and stitch ¼ inch from the sleeve edge. Turn to the wrong side, when the stitching line will appear as *a*, Fig. 11; then press down and slip-stitch or stitch in place, as at *b*.

To make a good hem finish, apply seam tape or ribbon on the top of the hem in the

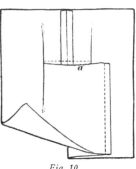

Fig. 10

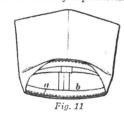

Fig. 11

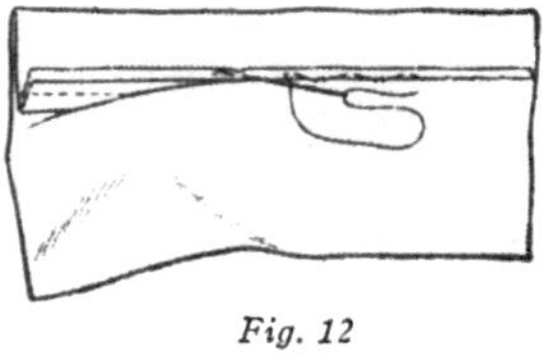

Fig. 12

same manner as for the sleeves. Then put the hem in with slip-stitches, taking up as little of the material of the dress as possible but making a secure stitch in the tape, as shown in Fig. 12.

Fig. 13

When fitting the dress, try on the collar that you choose to wear with it. Mark and cut the neck line that it requires, allowing for seams. Make sure that both sides of the neck are trimmed the same. Face the neck with a bias strip of silk or other suitable material. Sew two snap fasteners on the shoulder closing.

Making the Waist-Line Finish.—If a belt of the material is desired across the back, seam a 2-inch lengthwise strip together, using the pieces cut from the under-arm for this. Stitch the folded material the full length, about ¼ inch from the torn edge, and across one end, as in Fig. 13 (a). Turn the belt right side out. An easy way to do this is to place the blunt end of a pencil against the end seam and pull the belt down over the pencil, as in (b), until it is turned right side out. Then slip out the pencil. Press the belt and stitch across the open end.

If buckles are used, finish as shown in Fig. 1; otherwise, slip the ends of the belt strip underneath the front pinched-in plaits and secure them in place by means of ornamental buttons, tacking stitches, or machine stitching.

Complete the dress by pressing it and adding the collar and cuffs.

Cutting and Applying Long Sleeves

If long sleeves are desired, fold in the center, lengthwise, a piece of material as long as you want the sleeve and as wide as the armhole measure, as in Fig. 14. Measure down on the lengthwise edges 3½ inches, locating point a, and then draw a diagonal line from a to the end of the fold, b. This gives a pointed sleeve that will fit perfectly into the straight armhole, as shown in Fig. 15.

Baste the sleeve in the armhole and stitch in before the under-arm seams are stitched, as shown. Start at the shoulder seam, as at a, to baste and stitch so as to bring the point in exact position and avoid stretching either the sleeve or the material.

For long sleeves of this type, an effective wrist finish is shown in Fig. 16. Fit the sleeve at the wrist with pinched-in plaits and make a turn-over, center-stitched binding at the lower edge, as shown in Figs. 8 and 9, page 12.

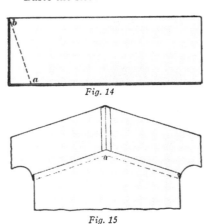

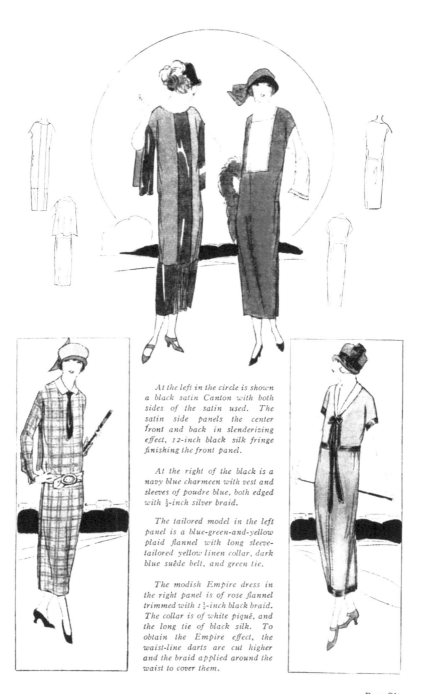

At the left in the circle is shown a black satin Canton with both sides of the satin used. The satin side panels the center front and back in slenderizing effect, 12-inch black silk fringe finishing the front panel.

At the right of the black is a navy blue charmeen with vest and sleeves of poudre blue, both edged with ½-inch silver braid.

The tailored model in the left panel is a blue-green-and-yellow plaid flannel with long sleeve-tailored yellow linen collar, dark blue suède belt, and green tie.

The modish Empire dress in the right panel is of rose flannel trimmed with 1½-inch black braid. The collar is of white piqué, and the long tie of black silk. To obtain the Empire effect, the waist-line darts are cut higher and the braid applied around the waist to cover them.

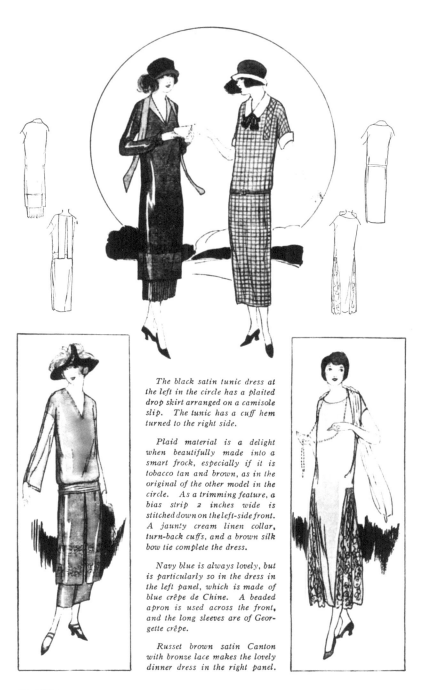

The black satin tunic dress at the left in the circle has a plaited drop skirt arranged on a camisole slip. The tunic has a cuff hem turned to the right side.

Plaid material is a delight when beautifully made into a smart frock, especially if it is tobacco tan and brown, as in the original of the other model in the circle. As a trimming feature, a bias strip 2 inches wide is stitched down on the left-side front. A jaunty cream linen collar, turn-back cuffs, and a brown silk bow tie complete the dress.

Navy blue is always lovely, but is particularly so in the dress in the left panel, which is made of blue crêpe de Chine. A beaded apron is used across the front, and the long sleeves are of Georgette crêpe.

Russet brown satin Canton with bronze lace makes the lovely dinner dress in the right panel.

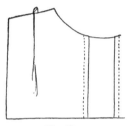 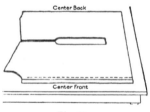

Fig. 17   Fig. 18   Fig. 19

Slenderizing One-Piece Dress

If the figure is larger than 40-inch bust and it is desired to use 54-inch material, buy one length plus ½ yard, and use ¼ yard to put a crosswise panel in the center front of the dress, as shown in Fig. 17. This panel may be stitched in crosswise tuck effect and used as a feature for a slenderizing dress. Or, if the hips are small in proportion to the bust, the panel may be omitted and a plain seam used and this covered with braid, as in Fig. 18. The seam may come at the center front or left-side front or right-side back. In any event, the panel or plain seam should be made complete before the dress is cut out.

Cutting Out the Dress.—Place the material, which is now in the form of a tube, lengthwise, so that the center of the panel makes one fold and this fold is toward you. Then fold the material in half lengthwise, turning the panel fold up, or away from you, when it will be in the position shown in Fig. 4, with the exception that there will be a fold where the selvages are shown, as this dress has no side seam. Then cut the dress out as explained and shown in Fig. 4. When the dress is cut and opened out, the upper part will appear as in Fig. 19.

Shoulder-Seam Dart.—If the bust is slightly full, and ease across the front is desired, or if plaids or checks are to be matched at the shoulder seam, a dart may be placed 1½ inches from the neck curve on each shoulder, as shown in Fig. 17. This may be pressed in ¾ inch deep (1½ inches altogether), and caught just at the shoulder seam, or it may be stitched down, dart fashion, for 2 or 3 inches.

Applying the Hip Plait and Belt Straps.—The plait at the side over the hips should be pressed back to form an inverted plait, thus making a box plait on the wrong side, as shown in Fig. 20, and an inverted plait on the right. Catch the box plait securely to the underarm seam with overcasting-stitches, as shown.

Fig. 20

To hold the belt in position, wee belt straps are secured in place from the right side just about the inverted box plait, as shown in Fig. 21. Cut these 1⅜ inches wide and 2 inches long, overcast the raw edges together, and press the straps carefully. Then tuck the ends under, pin the straps in place, as shown, and apply them to the dress by means of invisible stitches.

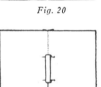

Fig. 21

The Two-Piece One Hour Dress

The type of One Hour Dress shown in Fig. 1, when attractively made of smart new material, is a joy to own. The fact that it is a little less tailored than the one-piece dress makes it more adaptable to a variety of fabrics, from wool to calico, from Swiss to chiffon; in fact, any fabric that does not have a definite nap, such as flat-pile velvet, broadcloth, or similar materials, can be used. Stripes are very smart for it, used lengthwise in the blouse and around in the skirt. Heavy silk crêpes and wash fabrics are ideal.

Measurements and Width of Materials

Take the measurements exactly the same as for the One-Piece One Hour Dress. See Page 1.

If you are more than a 38-inch bust, use 40-inch material. If you are less than 38, 36-inch material is satisfactory. And if you are less than 34, 32-inch material may be used. From 3 to 3½ yards of 36- or 40-inch material are required.

Fig. 1

If you are tall and slender, the only waste in cutting the dress will be that cut out in shaping the neck.

This type of dress is desirable for children, too. The measurements are taken in the same way as for an adult and the dress cut the same except that the neck is made smaller and a 4-inch opening made at the center back to allow the dress to slip over the head.

Dividing the Material

You now divide your material into two parts, one for the blouse and one for the skirt, as in Fig. 2.

Measure off from one end the *blouse length*, and place a pin in the edge of the material to mark the point. Clip through the selvage and cut or tear across. The shorter part is for the blouse; the longer part, for the skirt.

NOTE.—Some materials tear satisfactorily; others do not. The best way to make a crosswise division of material which does tear well is to clip through the selvage edge and tear across. If you prefer to cut it, draw a crosswise thread and cut on the drawn thread line. Materials that pull when torn or that are printed or shaped unevenly on the bolt are more satisfactorily divided by cutting.

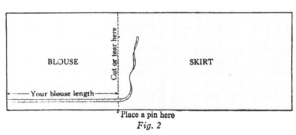

Fig. 2

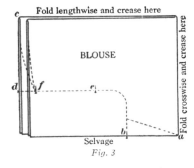

Fig. 3

Cutting Out the Blouse

Cutting the Armhole and Under Arm. Fold the shorter piece of material, or the blouse length, first lengthwise, selvage edges together, and then crosswise, as in Fig. 3. Bring one crosswise end up 1 inch to make the front longer than the back and allow for fulness over the bust. Measure to the left from the crosswise fold *a* along the selvage one-half the arm-hole measure and place a pin, as at *b*. Measure from the fold *c* one-fourth the hip measure plus 1½ inches and place a pin, as at *d*.

To obtain the armhole curve, measure straight to the right of *d* 8 or 10 inches and place a pin, as at *e*.

Next, cut straight in from *b*, turning as the pin at *e* is approached and making a smooth, even under-arm curve. Then continue to cut straight down from *e* to *d*, as shown by the dotted line.

Shaping the Waist Line and Sleeves.—To shape the waist line of the blouse, measure up from the bottom ½ to ⅝ inch and place a pin, as at *f*. On the upper piece, which is for the back, taper a curved line from *f* to a point halfway between the under arm and the lengthwise fold. For the front, cut in a curved line on the lower piece from *f* toward *c* to a point slightly more than half way, as shown.

If a pointed sleeve is desired, measure up 3½ inches from *b* on the sleeve line and then cut in a diagonal line from *a* to the 3½-inch point.

Cutting Out the Neck.—Now, to cut the neck, as in Fig. 4, open out the blouse on the crosswise fold and turn it so that the folded edge is toward you and the back or short part of the blouse, comes to your left. Measure up on the crosswise crease 4½ inches and mark with a pin, as at *a*. Measure 1 inch on the back fold from the crosswise crease and mark with a pin, as at *b*. Measure to the right from the crosswise crease 4½ inches and mark with a pin, as at *c*.

Cut the front-neck curve by cutting from *c* to *a* and the back curve by cutting from *b* to *a*.

Utilizing the Under-Arm Sections.—When the blouse is cut, it should appear as in Fig. 5, which shows also the sections cut out at the under arms. Use one of these sections for cutting 1½-inch bias binding for finishing the neck, the bottom of the sleeves, and the pockets, and the other for 6- by 9-inch pockets, as shown. Shape the flaps of the pockets if the sleeves have been shaped, but if they are straight, cut the pockets the same size but with a straight turn-over at the top.

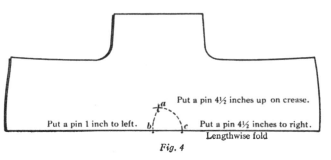

Fig. 4

If pockets are not desired and the sleeve is cut straight, the under-arm pieces may be used as straight cuffs to extend the length of the sleeve.

Proportioning the Skirt

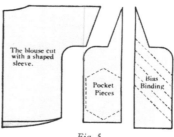

Fig. 5

You now cut the belt and skirt from the larger piece of material, as in Fig. 6. For the belt, measure 2½ inches from one selvage edge and cut a strip the full length of the material, cutting on a lengthwise thread. Measure the skirt length from the cut edge down toward the selvage. The material that remains may be used for a hem.

The skirt material should be wide enough to provide for the hip measure plus 6 inches for ease and 20 inches for plaits, each of the two large plaits taking up 8 inches, or 16 inches for both, and each of the four small plaits 1 inch, or 4 inches in all. Thus, if your hip measure is 40 inches, you will need 40 + 26, or 66 inches.

The dress is now cut and ready for stitching.

Making the Blouse

Binding the Neck.—The first step is to seam the binding strips to make a center-stitched binding for the neck. To do this, join two or three bias pieces, as in Fig. 7, by placing the lengthwise edges together, stitching in a ¼-inch seam, and pressing open with the fingers. Sometimes two and sometimes three pieces are required for the neck, as the length of the pieces depends on the width of the material and the size of the hip measure. Piecings are not objectionable in the bindings, providing the seams are carefully stitched, surplus edges trimmed away, and the seam then pressed open.

Bias bindings may be bought prepared ready for use. Some of these are lovely and many are made in organdie, lawn, and silk, so they are suitable for all fabrics. Hercules braid, also, is desirable as a finish for silk or wool tailored dresses. In using Hercules braid, fold it lengthwise and press it carefully before starting to apply it as binding. The crosswise ends will join more neatly if a row of machine stitching is placed across each one to avoid stretching.

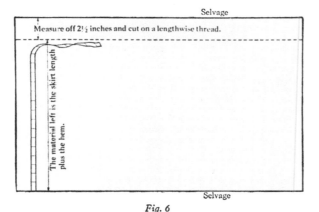

Fig. 6

Fig. 7

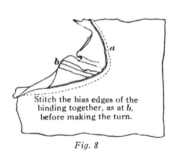

Fig. 8

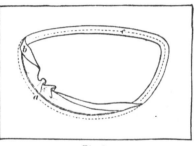

Fig. 9

Place the right side of the binding to the wrong side of the neck and stitch in a ¼-inch seam, as shown at *a*, Fig. 8. Begin stitching at one shoulder and stitch across the back of the neck and around toward the front. Do this easily and without stretching either the neck or the binding. Stitch all the way around and join the binding in a bias seam where it meets, as at *b*, that is, on a lengthwise thread, just as the other joinings were made.

Crease the binding on the under side up from the stitching line *a*, Fig. 9. Then turn the free edge of the binding over ⅜ inch, as at *b*, drawing the edge up smooth and even and creasing as straight as possible. Turn the creased edge *b* down well over the stitching line *a*, and stitch through the center, as at *c*. Begin the stitching at the shoulder and proceed around the back as before.

Finishing the Sleeves.—To bind the two sleeves, join three strips of the binding, open the seams, place the right side of the binding to the right side of the sleeve, as at *a*, Fig. 10, and stitch in a ¼-inch seam. Turn the binding to the wrong side and make a center-stitched binding. Turn back in cuff effect, as shown at *b*.

When the material is attractive on the wrong side, a turn-over center-stitched binding, as in Fig. 11, may be made from the sleeve itself or as a cuff finish without using a binding piece. To make this, turn ⅜ inch to ½ inch, as at *a*; then make another ½ inch turn, as at *b*. Stitch directly in the center. This will give the same effect as the center-stitched bias binding that is used at the neck.

When this finish is applied, as in a cuff or a cascade, turn the edges in at the corner in square effect and stitch, as at *c*.

Completing the Blouse.—With the sleeve finish completed, sew the under-arm seams, right sides together, for a French seam. Turn and complete the seams. At the bottom of the sleeves, turn and stitch back in the stitching line just made about 1 inch to secure the cuff edge and to stay the thread ends.

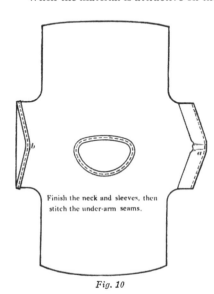

Fig. 10

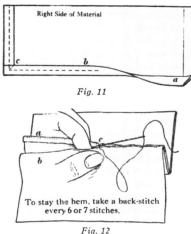

Fig. 11

Fig. 12

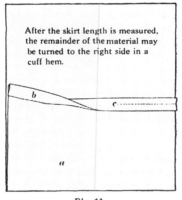

Fig. 13

Making the Skirt

Putting in the Hem.—Now, with the blouse stitched, proceed to make the skirt, which has just one seam. Before seaming it, decide on the hem finish. A plain hem may be turned and machine-stitched in or it may be slip-stitched, as in Fig. 12. Before slip-stitching a hem, first turn the top of the hem edge down $\frac{1}{4}$ inch, as at a, and stitch by machine. This gives a firm edge that will aid in keeping a straight line and also protect the slip-stitches. To slip-stitch easily, hold the skirt side next to you, as at b, having the fingers on the hem side. Take up as little material with each stitch as possible. To avoid pulling or puckering the hemming-stitches, hold the hem secure and take a back-stitch every six or seven stitches, as at c.

A simple yet smart and attractive finish and an excellent substitute for a hand hem is the cuff hem shown in Fig. 13. This should be put in before the skirt seam is stitched.

To make a cuff hem, turn the hem portion to the right side, as at a, creasing on a lengthwise thread. Turn the edge over $\frac{3}{8}$ inch, as at b, and turn the fold $\frac{1}{2}$ inch, as at c. Press down and stitch directly in the center.

Seaming the Skirt.—If a cuff hem is used, prepare to French seam the skirt, as in Fig. 14. Pin the bottom a and top b of the hem ends together so that they will be perfectly even and cannot slip during the stitching.

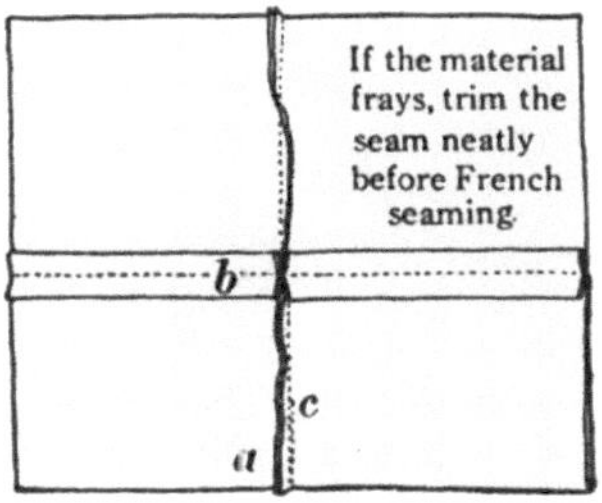

Fig. 14

Contrary to the regular rule, begin the stitching of the skirt at the bottom. Stay the end of the seam by beginning 1 inch from the bottom, as at c, stitching to the bottom, and then turning and stitching the full length of the seam. Turn wrong side out and complete the French seam, remembering to stay each end.

If you desire, the hem may be omitted and binding or braid used to finish the bottom of the skirt.

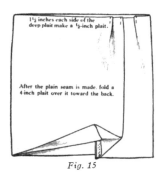

Fig. 15

Joining the Skirt and Blouse

Putting in the Skirt Plaits.—Lay a 4-inch plait on one side of the skirt, having the seam come at the inside of the plait, as shown in Fig. 15. This plait may be laid toward the back or the front, as desired, and should be pressed in straight from top to bottom of the skirt.

About $1\frac{1}{2}$ inches each side of this plait, lay a small plait, about $\frac{1}{2}$ inch deep, as shown, to take up all extra fulness. As both sides are alike, measure half way around the skirt and pin three similar plaits in the opposite side. The edges of each deep plait should come at the under-arm seam of the waist.

If the figure is full across the back in the hips, an inverted plait, with each plait made 2 inches deep and edges turned to meet, is more satisfactory than the deep 4-inch plait.

If soft material, such as crêpe, is used, the sides may be shirred in instead of plaited, as shown in Fig. 16, five or six rows of shirring placed 1 inch apart being desirable. When gathered up, the shirring should take in the allowance of the plaits on each side. A loose, long machine stitch permits a quick, satisfactory shirring. The thread ends of the shirring should be secured with a needle.

Making the Waist-Line Joining.—Next, proceed to pin the skirt to the waist, as shown in Fig. 17, having the edges of the deep plaits, if they are used, meet the under-arm seams. Determine at this time whether you want the plaits to turn to the front or the back. Slip the skirt over the waist with the waist-line edges together, and hold the dress so that you pin the blouse to the skirt, thus preventing its being drawn too tight.

To the notched center front and center back of the waist, pin the centers of the front and the back of the skirt, and place several pins in between these points. By easing in the waist material, the skirt should fit on very well, but if necessary the plaits may be adjusted slightly.

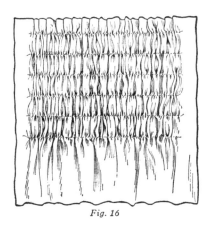

Fig. 16

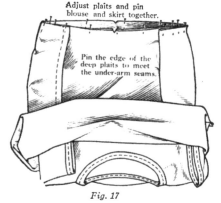

Fig. 17

Page Fifteen

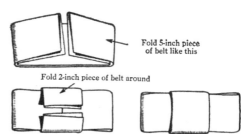

Fig. 18

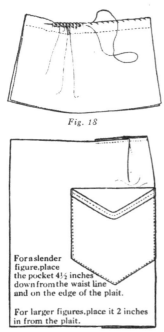

For a slender figure, place the pocket 4½ inches down from the waist line and on the edge of the plait.

For larger figures, place it 2 inches in from the plait.

Fig. 19

Fold 5-inch piece of belt like this

Fold 2-inch piece of belt around

Fig. 20

When the waist and skirt are pinned together, stitch all the way around by machine, using a ⅜-inch seam and overlapping the stitching for a couple of inches. Then overcast the raw edges, as in Fig. 18, taking up a number of stitches at one time in order to do the work quickly.

For materials that are too heavy to French seam, overcast the other seams by means of this group overcasting, as shown.

Making the Pocket and Belt

If pockets are used, finish the upper edge with a center-stitched binding, as in Fig. 19. Turn the lap over to the right side and pin the pockets accurately in position, turning in the edges ⅜ inch. Begin ½ inch from the top, stitch to the top, and then back to stay the top edge securely.

Make the belt as explained for the One-Piece Dress. Then, to make a tailored bow for the belt, cut off a piece of the belt material 5 inches long. Fold the ends to meet in the center, as shown in Fig. 20, and tack down. Cut off another piece 2 inches long, fold this around the first piece at the center, as shown, and tack down.

Sew the tailored bow to one end of the finished belt. If the belt will slip over your shoulders, sew both ends of the belt to the bow. If not, put snap fasteners on the belt. Secure the bow just in front of the left-side seam.

Variations of the Two-Piece Dress

In the circle at the left on Page 15 is shown a green-and-blue, even-plaid taffeta with true bias skirt, bias ruffle trimming for neck and sleeves, and a center-stitched binding as a finish for the bottom. The blouse is in basque effect.

At the upper right, flat crêpe and pearl trimming make a lovely evening dress.

At the left center is a russet brown flannel with crêpe sleeves and tie and novelty braid trimming.

Erect-pile velvet, metallic cloth, and fur make the full-skirt basque frock shown at the right center.

At the lower left is shown wool and silk in an attractive combination.

The frock at the lower right is suitable in design for afternoon or evening. The blouse fulness at the waist line is held in with pinched-in plaits. The skirt is cut as if a 4-inch plait were to be used at each side but of a full width of material. The extra width makes the turnover at the waist line, and the plait material, the cascade.

Home of the Woman's Institute

Learn at Home to Make All Your Own Clothes

THE "One Hour Dress" was created by Mary Brooks Picken, Director of Instruction of the Woman's Institute of Domestic Arts and Sciences. This great school at Scranton, Pa., is the largest school of dressmaking and designing in the world and teaches exclusively by the home study method.

Mrs. Picken created the "One Hour Dress" especially to demonstrate how easily you can make attractive clothes when you have proper instructions. The directions in this book are just an example of the amazingly simple methods used in the Woman's Institute new Course in Dressmaking and Designing.

This new Course presents an entirely new way of learning to make your own clothes, based on the Institute's successful experience in teaching more than 200,000 women and girls. It is a new method by which you start at once to make actual garments, a new plan so fascinating that you will want to spend every spare moment in planning and making the many pretty clothes you have always wanted, but never felt you could afford to buy.

By this new method, you, too, can now quickly learn in spare time, in your own home, to make all your own clothes, or you can prepare to take up Dressmaking as a business—secure a good-paying position or open a shop of your own.

It costs you nothing to find out all about the Woman's Institute and what it can do for you. Just send a letter, post card, or the convenient card enclosed and you will receive, without obligation, the full story of this great school and just how it can help you. Please state whether most interested in home or professional dressmaking.

Woman's Institute
Dept. 410, Scranton, Pa.

CPSIA information can be obtained
at www.ICGtesting.com
Printed in the USA
JSHW041131040323
38332JS00017B/6